AI For Beginners Over Fifty: The Companion Workbook

Practice Prompts, Hands-On Exercises and Progress Reflection to Build Confidence in AI and Streamline Your Daily Life

Margaret Fields

1957 Publishing

This Book Belongs To: ______________________

Book Cover Designed By: Margaret Fields

1st Edition: 2025

About The Author

Margaret Fields

At 67 years young, Margaret Fields is a proud senior, a devoted mother of three, and a loving grandmother to four. Her journey began at St Patrick's Business College, where she earned the distinguished title of Dux at just 17 years old. Margaret has witnessed the remarkable evolution of technology, from the introduction of electric golf-ball typewriters in the early 70s to her first encounter with an IBM Memory Typewriter in 1977. The mid-90s brought her first computer, a model 186, sparking a lifelong passion for technology. In 2011, Margaret's business imported Australia's first 7-axis robotic stone milling machine, further deepening her love for innovation. With a Master of Arts with excellence from the University of New South Wales, she proudly embraces her identity as a neurodivergent thinker. Her self-taught journey through IT has been fueled by a desire for age-appropriate and structured learning materials, ultimately inspiring her to write this book.

Dedication

To My Study Buddy

To Mooie, my beloved and irreplaceable Study Buddy. Through the trials of my cancer treatment in 2013 and the countless hours of my Master of Arts journey at the University of NSW, Mooie was a constant source of comfort and strength. Though she has now passed, her spirit continues to inspire and guide me. To you, dear reader, I invite you to think of Mooie as your own Study Buddy. Please give her a virtual pat and head rub whenever you seek encouragement. Let her enduring legacy support you on your journey.

"Mooie"

There once was a Tech-savvy Dream. Where AI was more than it seemed.

Before the folks understood, They wondered whether they should,

Trust in this crazy new scheme. Then came this book, wise and true,

With guidance on what they should do. Their fears turn to cheers,

As wisdom appears, AI became friend, not taboo!

So here's to the Fifty-Plus crew, Embracing this tech that's so new.

With humor and grace, They keep up the pace,

And AI they now all pursue!

By Margaret Fields

Contents

Introduction

Welcome to Your Companion Workbook: A Gentle Beginning

Have you ever stared down at your phone and thought, **"When did this thing get smarter than me?"** Or squinted at a screen full of symbols, abbreviations, and flashing buttons, wondering if you'd somehow stumbled into a spaceship control panel?

You're not alone.

Seventy-three percent of adults over fifty admit they feel overwhelmed by the rapid pace of technological advancements. It's like we've been dropped into a foreign country without a map, a compass, or even a helpful tour guide. No wonder our hair goes grey (and occasionally migrates south).

But here's the good news: This workbook is your friendly guide - and your space to think, reflect, learn, and maybe even laugh a little along the way. Think of it as your **AI adventure journal**: a place where you can scribble your thoughts, answer simple prompts, color a few calming mandalas, and slowly but surely build your confidence.

From One Learner to Another...

When I started exploring AI, I had no clue what a chatbot was and nearly flung my phone across the room the first time it talked back to me.

But here's the thing: I kept going. I leaned into curiosity instead of fear. And now? I want you to experience that same sense of discovery - without the overwhelm.

You don't have to be a tech expert. You don't even have to be "good at computers." You just need a sense of humor, a bit of patience, and this workbook.

What You'll Find Inside

This workbook follows along with the main book, AI For Beginners Over Fifty. You'll find:

- **Sticky Note-To-Self reminders** to nudge and encourage you
- **Simple prompts and exercises** to help you reflect and practice
- **Creative mandala coloring pages** to give your brain a break
- **Room to explore** what this new world of AI might offer you
- And a few gentle surprises tucked in along the way

Whether you're here to learn how to talk to a voice assistant, understand what "the cloud" really means, or just prove to your grandkids that you're not stuck in the Stone Age, you're in the right place.

Why This Workbook Matters

This isn't just about learning a new skill. It's about **reshaping the narrative** - about yourself, about aging, and about your place in a world that's rapidly changing.

You're not behind. You're just getting started. And I'll be right here with you.

So sharpen your pencil, warm up that cup of tea (or something more substantial - I won't tell), and settle in. Let's make this journey into AI feel like a **comfortable conversation**, not a crash course.

Together, we'll explore, practice, color, and celebrate every small step.

Now, turn the page, and let the adventure begin!

With you all the way,

Margaret

(Your ever-curious, slightly cheeky guide to all things AI)

Everyday AI, Demystified

Let's Start with a Little Story of Your Own

Have you ever caught yourself talking to a machine - like the microwave or remote control? Tell the story! What were you asking it to do? Did it “respond”?

- **What’s a moment when technology made you laugh (or sigh in relief)?** Describe a small but meaningful way AI has already snuck into your life.

Understanding AI, One Task at a Time

- **In your own words, how would you describe Artificial Intelligence to a curious friend?** (Don’t worry about being technical - just keep it real.)

- **List 3 things in your daily life that likely use AI (even if you didn’t realize it before).** Hint: Think phones, emails, online shopping, voice assistants...

- **Which AI feature do you enjoy the most? Which one annoys or confuses you?** Share why. (Yes, even if it’s those “helpful” ads that follow you around.

Smart but Not Sentient

- **What’s one common fear or myth you’ve heard about AI? Do you still believe it? Why or why not?**

- **How does it feel to learn that AI doesn't think, feel, or judge - especially not your podcast choices?** Be honest. (Some of us do like listening to "Love in the golden years.")

AI That Works for You

- **Imagine your perfect AI assistant. What tasks would it handle for you each day?** (Laundry folding? Doctor's appointment reminders? Telling the grandkids it's bedtime?)

- **What's one daily habit or task you wish were easier? Could AI help with that?**

- **Do you currently use a smart home device? If yes, how do you feel about it? If not, would you ever try one? Why or why not?**

Machine Learning: Like a DJ with a Good Memory

- **What kind of music or product suggestions do you get online? Are they "spot on" or hilariously off?** Share an example.

- **Think about learning something new - like a language, skill, or recipe.** Now, think of AI doing the same thing with data.What does that comparison help you understand about machine learning?

- **If you could train a machine to learn** one thing about you perfectly**, what would it be?**

Neural Networks: A Digital Brain in Action

- **This part might've sounded technical. What part of the "neural network" explanation stood out to you the most?** (Was it the detective metaphor, the layered brain visual, or something else?)

- **What surprised you about where neural networks are used (e.g., in medicine or translation)?** Which application excites or intrigues you most?

- **Do you feel more or less confident about understanding how AI makes decisions now? Why?**

Everyday AI: Your Voice, Their Ears

- **If you could only ask your voice assistant** one thing **each day - what would it be?** (Be as specific, silly, or serious as you like.)

- **What's one way a smart device has (or could) make your life easier at home?**

- **Do you feel comfortable managing your smart device's privacy settings?** Why or why not? What would help you feel more secure?

Looking Ahead

- **Which part of this chapter made you feel the most curious? The most confident?** Reflect on what you've learned.

- **What's one small action you'd like to try next to explore AI more intentionally?** (It could be as simple as asking Siri to remind you to water the plants.)

Smart Home With AI

Prompt: Take a moment to reflect on your current home setup. Which of the following smart home features are you already using, and which ones are you curious to try?

- Smart thermostat
- Automated lighting
- Smart locks or cameras
- Voice assistant (e.g., Alexa, Siri, Google)
- Appliance scheduling (e.g., smart plugs, robot vacuums)
- Other:

Guided Question: What is one small smart upgrade you could make this month to improve comfort, security, or energy efficiency?

Smart-Home Security Checklist

Use this page to ensure your smart home setup is safe and secure.

- Strong passwords set for all smart devices
- Multifactor authentication enabled
- All devices are connected to a secure, encrypted network
- Automatic software updates are turned ON
- Regular privacy checkups scheduled (monthly or quarterly)

Reflection: What one action from this list can you complete today to better protect your smart home?

Voice Assistant Confidence Builder

Activity: Choose one of the following tasks and try it using your voice assistant.

- Add a calendar event
- Set a reminder
- Ask for the weather
- Request a joke
- Start a playlist or podcast

Journal Prompt: How did it feel to interact with your voice assistant in this way? Did anything surprise or impress you?

Meal Planner Exercise: AI in the Kitchen

Step 1: Pick an AI-powered meal planning app (like Whisk, Yummly, or a smart fridge companion app).

Step 2: Enter your dietary preference or goal for the week (e.g., heart-healthy, gluten-free).

Step 3: Let the App generate a meal plan.

Prompt: Write down your favorite suggested meal and the ingredients you'll need:

Meal Name:

Ingredients:

One thing that made this easier than usual:

AI Shopping List Assistant

Activity: Use a digital list builder or AI assistant to prepare your grocery list.

- Add 3 items from your pantry inventory
- Have it suggest 2 meal ideas based on what you already have
- Let it recommend a substitute for an item you don't have

Reflection: Was your list more accurate or helpful than usual? What tool did you use?

Smart Travel Prep Sheet

Scenario Prompt: You're planning a weekend getaway using an AI-powered travel app.

Where are you going?

App used:

Bonus Tip: List two safety measures you'll take while traveling with AI support:

Financial Tracker & Goal Setter

Exercise: Pick a financial AI app (like PocketGuard, Cleo, or your bank's built-in AI) and do the following:

- Track your spending for one category (e.g., dining out)
- Set one savings goal
- Check your credit score if the App allows it

Workbook Prompt: What's one financial insight you discovered? How could you change a habit this month?

Personal AI Setup Plan

Guided Questions:

- What's one area of life where you'd love less friction or more support? e.g., remembering appointments, tracking health, saving money
- Which AI tool could help? If unsure, jot down a few ideas based on this chapter.
- What's one small experiment you'll try this week with AI?

Staying Connected with AI

Connecting Through AI – Family, Friends & Community

Staying Social with AI-Powered Tools

Have you ever received a perfectly timed photo notification or tagged post that made your day? ___________Write about the moment and how it made you feel.

What are your favorite kinds of social media content?

- Family photos
- Recipe videos
- Travel inspiration
- Funny animals
- Other:

Does your feed ever feel like it's "reading your mind"? _______________ Why do you think that happens?

Have you ever noticed a post that upset you - or seemed to appear too often? ____________ What do you think AI might have learned to send that content your way?

Chatbots, Tone & Sentiment: Talking With AI

Have you ever used a chatbot (on social media, a shopping site, or elsewhere)?

- Yes – it was helpful
- Yes – it was confusing
- No – I avoid them

Write a quick note about how you felt using it:

How important is it to you that online conversations "feel positive"? ____________________ What do you think about platforms using AI to keep things kind?

Privacy and AI on Social Media

On a scale of 1 to 5, how confident are you in managing your social media privacy settings?

- 1 – Not confident at all
- 2
- 3
- 4
- 5 – I've got it covered

Have you ever updated your settings to control who sees your posts or tags? _____________ What changes did you make (or would like to make)?

AI can alert you to suspicious activity. Would you feel safer knowing this is happening quietly in the background? ________________ Why or why not?

Photo Tagging & Content Curation

Think of a moment when AI helped organize your photos or family memories. Did it feel magical... or mildly creepy?

If your social media feed could be curated just for you - what would you want more of? List 3 topics or types of posts you'd love to see.

Video Calls & Virtual Meetups: AI Makes It Seamless

What frustrates you the most about video calls?

- Background noise
- Poor video quality
- Tech issues
- Forgetting when the call is

Now, list 1 or 2 things you've noticed getting better thanks to AI.

- Have you ever used:
- Noise cancellation?
- Real-time translation?

- Closed captioning?

Which would be most helpful for your next virtual chat?

If you could add one magical AI feature to your video calls, what would it be?

Let AI Help With Virtual Events

Imagine AI handled your next family or community video event. Which tasks would you hand over?

- Sending invites
- Finding a good time
- Setting reminders
- Creating a background
- Tech support

What's one tip you'd give someone nervous about trying their first video meetup?

AI in Genealogy: Finding Your Roots

Have you ever explored your family history? ______________ What did you discover - or what questions do you still have?

Which of these genealogy tools sounds exciting to try?

- Facial recognition in old family photos

- AI-assisted family tree builders
- Historical record matchups
- Story verification (Did Great-Uncle Alf really race camels?)

Share a family story (even if it's a bit fuzzy) that you'd love to investigate.

Building Community with AI Platforms

Would you enjoy a digital platform that suggests groups, clubs, or events based on your hobbies? ____________ Why or why not?

If AI could introduce you to 3 people who share your interests, what interests would you want it to match you on?

Have you ever used a local group, app, or online space to stay involved in your community?

If not - what would make you want to start?

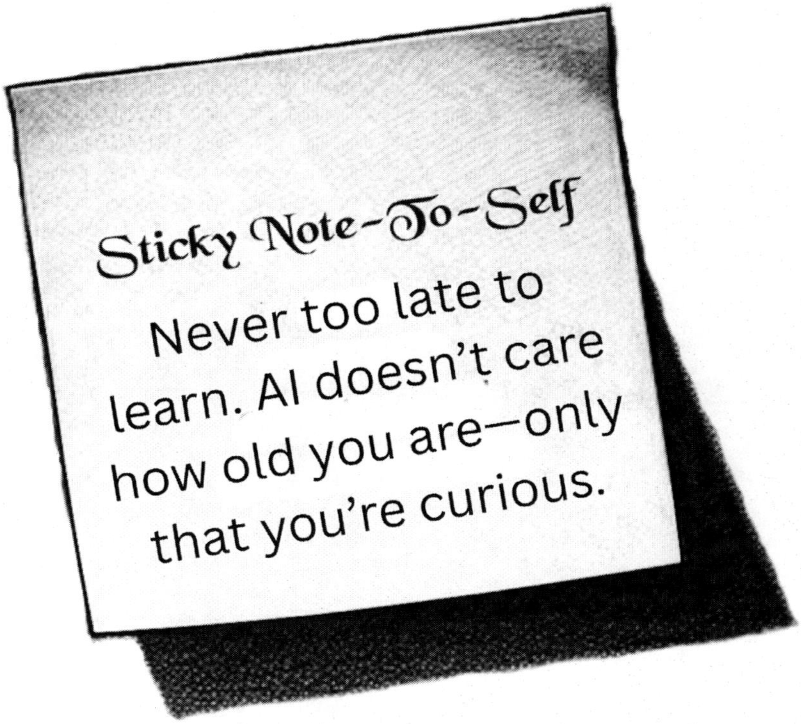

Wrap-Up Reflection

Which section of this chapter surprised you the most?

Why?

What's one AI tool you'd like to explore this month to help you stay connected?

Health & Wellness with AI

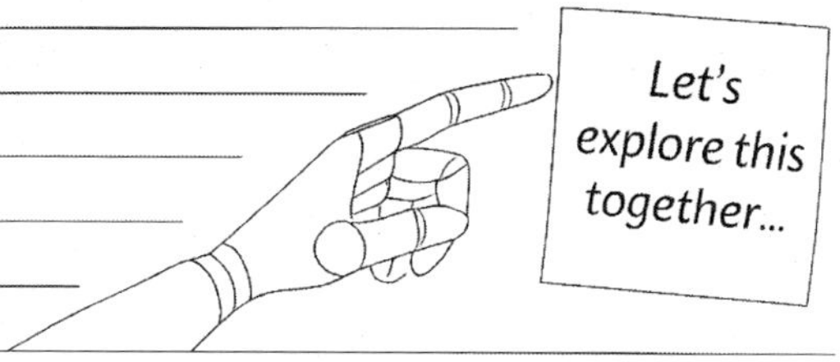

AI & Your Health – One Gentle Step at a Time

Wearable Tech: Tracking Your Wellness with a Wink and a Beep

What wearable device (if any) do you currently use - or have you considered using?

- Fitness tracker
- Smartwatch
- Health patch
- None yet, but I'm curious!

What's something your wearable has tracked that surprised or amused you? (e.g., your heart rate during a dramatic movie or your sleep habits)

How do you feel when your device celebrates a goal?

Describe that moment - was it motivating, or did it make you roll your eyes a bit?

What kind of reminders would you enjoy from a health device?

- Move/stretch reminders
- Breathing exercises
- Water intake

- Kind encouragement
- Warnings about unexpected obstacles (like... dog poop)

Remote Monitoring: Care from the Couch

If you had a health device that sent updates to your doctor or family, what would you want it to track?

- Blood pressure
- Glucose levels
- Heart rate
- Other:

Would knowing your vitals were being monitored behind the scenes give you peace of mind - or make you feel watched?

Share your honest thoughts.

What kind of AI "health alert" would make you feel most supported - not stressed?

Medication Management: No More Guessing Games

Do you ever forget to take your medication?

- Rarely
- Sometimes
- All the time

What system (if any) do you currently use to manage your meds?

- Pillbox
- Calendar
- Phone alarm
- AI app/dispenser
- Other:

What would your dream medication assistant do for you? (e.g., sort pills, send reminders, check for bad combinations)

What message would make you smile if it popped up as a reminder? Write your own fun or kind alert line.

Personalized Fitness: Your Digital Trainer With No Yelling

What are your top 2 fitness goals right now?

- Build strength
- Walk more
- Improve balance
- Increase flexibility
- Maintain energy
- Just move my body more!

What type of exercise do you most enjoy or feel safe trying?

How would you like your AI trainer to “talk” to you?

- Calm and encouraging
- Cheeky and fun
- Short and clear
- Motivational speaker vibes

Optional: Write a message you’d love to hear after a workout.

Think of one small milestone you could celebrate this week. What is it?

Mental Wellness & Mindfulness: Finding Your Digital Zen

Have you ever tried a mindfulness or meditation app?

- Yes, and I loved it
- Yes, but I forgot about it
- No, but I’m curious
- Nope - not my thing

What time of day might be easiest for a 5-minute pause just for you?

- Morning
- Midday
- Evening

- Bedtime

What kind of calming support would you appreciate from an app?

- Mood tracking
- Guided meditations
- Gratitude prompts
- Breathing exercises
- Soft music or nature sounds

Describe how you'd like to feel after using a relaxation app. Write one sentence or a few keywords.

Reflection: A Healthier Life With a Little AI Help

Of all the tools in this chapter - wearables, health monitors, medication apps, fitness plans, and mindfulness helpers - which one feels the most exciting or helpful to you right now?

What's one small action you can take this week to explore or set up an AI health tool? (e.g., downloading a tracker app, setting a hydration reminder, asking someone about their smartwatch)

What message would you write to your future self about taking care of your health - gently, wisely, and with a sense of humor?

Privacy & Ethical Concerns

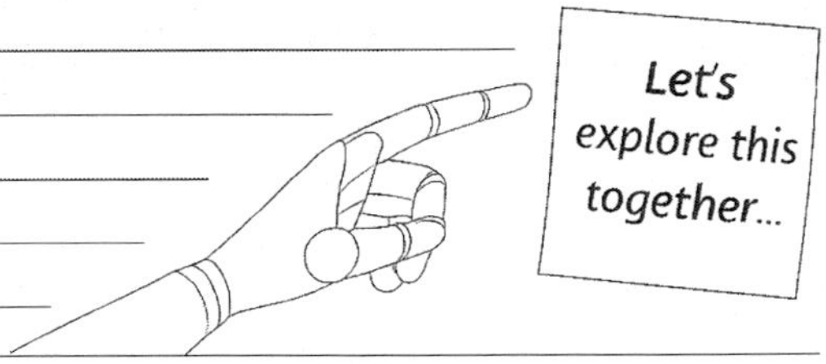

Guarding Your Digital Home & Playing Fair With AI

"That Ad Is Watching Me!" - Data Privacy Basics

Remember the last time an eerily perfect ad popped up? Describe what it was and how it made you feel.

On a scale of 1 (high) to 5 (low), how exposed do your online habits feel right now?

List three bits of personal info you'd never **hand to a stranger - but might already be handing to apps.**

Locking the Door – Tools & Habits

Which of these privacy tools have you tried?

- VPN
- Encrypted messaging
- Two-factor authentication
- None - teach me!

Pick one tool above (or another). What's your next step to start or improve it this week?

Password spring-clean: Write ONE password you'll update to something stronger (don't write the actual password - just which account!).

Fair Cake or Lopsided Slice? – Ethical AI & Bias

Think of a decision an AI system might make about you (loan offer, job ad, playlist). What could be unfair about that decision? ____ What would "fair" look like?

Have you ever felt left out or misjudged by tech? _____ Share the story – big or small.

If you could add one "fairness ingredient" to every algorithm, what would it be?

Know Your Rights – Regulations in Plain English

Match the right with the feeling: Digital Right | Why It Matters to YOU

Access my data |

Delete my data ("Right to be forgotten") |

Stop my data being sold |

Move my info elsewhere |

Which right above would you exercise first if it were easy?

Why?

Everyday Safe-Tech Checklist

App permission audit: Pick ONE app you use daily. Note any permission you'll revoke today.

App: ______________________________

Permission to remove:

Smart gadget sanity: Device you own (e.g., smart speaker): ______________ Feature you'll disable or secure:

Community watch: Where will you go for ongoing safety tips?

- Online forum
- Newsletters
- Friend/Grand-kid tutor
- Other:

Reflection & Action

Biggest "aha!" from this chapter?

Tiny habit you'll adopt this week for safer, fairer tech use:

AI & The Future of Life as We Know It

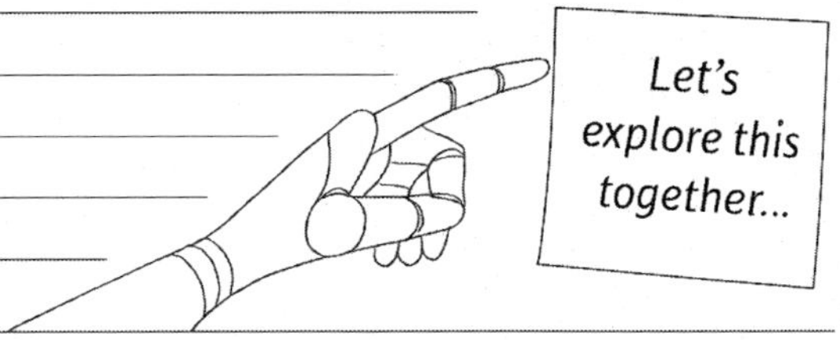

The Future of AI in Healthcare - Tailored, Predictive, and Precise

Imagine your doctor uses AI to match you with the right treatment based on your genetics.

How would that change how you feel about medical care?

Which future health tool sounds most helpful to you right now?

- Personalized medications
- Early-warning health forecasts
- AI-assisted surgery
- Super-fast diagnostics

What concerns (if any) would you want to be addressed before trying AI-powered healthcare?

AI in Transportation - From Hands-Free Rides to Traffic Harmony

Would you ever ride in a driverless car?

- Yes, bring it on
- Maybe, if I trusted it
- Only if I could sit in the driver's seat... just in case
- Nope, not for me

Which innovation would make your daily transport life better?

- Fewer red lights
- Safer intersections
- Efficient deliveries
- Greener travel options

If AI managed your travel routine for a week, what would you want it to do?

Smart Cities - A Day in an Intelligent Neighborhood

Picture your ideal “smart city” feature:

What’s one way AI could improve your neighborhood or town?

Which AI-powered public service do you think would help most?

- Smarter garbage collection
- AI-coordinated buses or trains
- Safer street surveillance
- Energy-saving buildings

Imagine your building or home adapted to your needs automatically.

What would it do first?

Environmental AI - Protecting the Planet with Data & Drones

What part of environmental protection feels most urgent to you?

- Wildlife conservation
- Climate change solutions
- Smarter agriculture
- Clean energy & water management

Which AI image sticks in your mind the most from this chapter?

- A drone over the savannah?
- A solar forecast?
- A digital farmer?

Do you believe AI can truly help save the planet?

- Yes
- MaybeI want to believe
- Only if we use it wisely

Looking Ahead - Your Thoughts on the Future

Which AI innovation in this chapter made you feel the most hopeful?

Why?

Which one made you pause or raise a concern?

If you could design your own AI tool to improve life in the future, what would it do?

Optional Bonus Activity: "One Day in a Future Powered by AI..."

Imagine your life in ten years with AI helping behind the scenes.

- Your morning routine
- How you get around
- Your health care
- Your environment

Write a short paragraph or a few playful bullet points that paint the picture.

Future Trends & Innovations in AI

Let AI Lighten the Load – Productivity, Balance & Free Time

AI for Efficient Task Management

What task do you most often forget or wish someone else would remind you to do?

If you had a digital assistant like Todoist or Trello, what's one recurring task you'd automate first?

- Take medication
- Water plants
- Call a friend
- Pay a bill
- Other:

On a scale of 1–5, how confident do you feel managing tasks with a digital tool?

- 1 – Not confident
- 2
- 3 – Somewhat comfortable
- 5 – I'm ready!

Automating Routine Tasks With AI Tools

Which "mundane" task takes up too much of your time lately?

Which of these sounds most helpful to try next?

- Email filtering
- Automatic document sorting
- Birthday reminders
- Monthly bill pay
- Smart grocery list

What's one benefit you'd hope to gain by automating more of your day? (e.g., "more mental clarity," "less stress in the mornings," etc.)

AI-Powered Time Tracking & Planning

What's your biggest "time sink" right now?

- Social media scrolling
- Email overload
- Multitasking
- TV or streaming
- Other:

If an AI tool helped you reclaim 1 hour per day, how would you spend that extra time?

How often do you plan breaks, hobbies, or creative time into your calendar?

- Never
- Occasionally
- Only on weekends
- I schedule them intentionally

Balancing Work & Leisure With AI

Describe your ideal day with a perfect balance of productivity and relaxation:

Morning:

Afternoon:

Evening:

Which part of your day could most benefit from a little AI help?

Let's dream a little - what kind of leisure activity would you love more time for?

- Painting or crafting
- Walks or gardening
- Reading
- Travel or day trips
- New hobby:

Reclaiming Free Time Through AI Efficiency

What small household or work task could you delegate to AI right now?

Which lifestyle improvement would bring you the most joy?

- More time with loved ones
- Starting a new hobby
- Less daily stressImproved sleep
- Other:

Create your "Reclaimed Time" Plan:

This week I'll reclaim ______ **minutes/hours** by letting AI handle ____________________________, so I can instead enjoy ____.

Personal Action Plan: Try, Tweak, Enjoy

Which AI tool or technique from this chapter would you like to try first?

What will help you stick with it for at least one week?

What's one word to describe how you want to feel about your time and tasks in the coming month?

- Clear
- Calm
- Energized
- In control

- Joyful
- Other: __________

Personal Growth with AI

Grow, Create & Learn - With a Little Help from AI

Learn Something New (From Your Couch)

What's one skill or hobby you've always wanted to try?

Which AI-powered learning tool would you most like to explore?

- Duolingo (languages)
- Rosetta Stone (languages with pronunciation help)
- Yousician (music)
- Other: ______________________

What appeals to you most about using an AI app to learn something new?

- Privacy and comfortInstant feedback
- Flexible timing
- Feels like a game!

Set your first mini-goal: I'd like to learn ____ for _______ minutes/day, __________ days/week.

Lifelong Learning Just for You

What kind of courses would you love to explore on platforms like GetSetUp or SeniorPlanet?

- Photography
- Technology skills

- Wellness
- History or Art
- Finance or digital safety
- Other:

What's your preferred learning pace?

- Fast and focused
- Gentle and flexible
- Somewhere in between

Who would you enjoy learning alongside?

- Solo with an appIn a small online group
- With a friend or family member

Learning Goal Setting: I want to learn about ______________________________ because ______________________________.

AI for Creativity (Art & Writing)

What kind of creativity calls to you most right now?

- Drawing or painting
- Photo transformation
- Writing stories or journaling
- Digital collage or design

Which creative AI tool are you curious to try?

- DeepArt – turning photos into famous art styles
- Artbreeder – blending and evolving images
- Grammarly – writing support
- AI story or poetry prompt generators

Write a short creative challenge for yourself using AI this week: "I will create ____________ using _______________ for fun and inspiration."

How would you describe your creative style in three words?

____________________ __________________ __________________ .

AI in Gardening – Tech with a Green Thumb

What kind of garden do you care for (or wish you did)?

- Pots on the porch
- Herb window box
- Veggie garden
- Flower beds
- Native plants & trees
- Still dreaming about it...

Which AI gardening helper would make your life easier?

- Plant ID app (like PlantSnap)
- Smart watering schedule

- Tailored plant care reminders
- Weather-based irrigation

Describe one current garden challenge you'd like help with:

Would you like to create garden "zones" with personalized care?

- Yes – sounds helpful!
- Maybe laterI'll stick with a watering can for now

Reflection: You, Learning, and the Journey Ahead

What's one unexpected thing you learned about yourself while reading this chapter?

What feels more possible now that you've explored how AI can help with personal growth?

If you could ask AI for help with one personal growth goal today, what would it be?

Hands on with AI Projects

Crafting Your Chatbot

Prompt 1: If your chatbot had a personality, how would you describe it in three words?

Prompt 2: What's one task you'd love a chatbot to handle for you – at home or online?

Prompt 3: Which platform are you curious to try first? (e.g., Dialogflow, Botpress, or other)

Building Your Smart Home

Prompt 4: Which smart feature would most improve your daily routine?

Prompt 5: Which devices do you already own that could be connected to a smart hub?

Prompt 6: What's your comfort level with starting a smart home setup?

- Curious
- Cautious
- Confident

AI Photography Fun

Prompt 7: What's your favorite photo subject - and how do you want AI to help you enhance it?

Prompt 8: Which AI photo editing feature excites you most? (e.g., auto-background removal, color correction, mood filters)

Prompt 9: Start your own photo style challenge! What 3 words describe the vibe you want your photos to express?

DIY AI Projects

Prompt 10: Which idea excites you more: an AI garden helper or an AI music curator - and why?

Prompt 11: What personal routine would you love to automate using a DIY AI setup?

Prompt 12: What materials or tools do you already have on hand to get started?

Family AI Activities

Prompt 13: Which family project sounds more fun - AI trivia night or a shared AI art mural?

Prompt 14: Who in your family would love this kind of project mostm - and what could be their special role?

Prompt 15: What would your family's first AI club project be?

Conclusion

You Did It! A Joyful Farewell (For Now)

Well, look at you! Pen in hand, thoughts on paper, and perhaps a few colored mandalas sprinkled in along the way... you've just completed your workbook journey through AI For Beginners Over Fifty - and what a journey it's been!

You started this adventure with curiosity (and maybe a raised eyebrow or two). Now you're standing here with a notebook full of insights, ideas, reflections - and proof that, **yes, you can absolutely learn something new, no matter your age or tech background**.

This workbook wasn't about "keeping up" with technology. It was about slowing down long enough to let **you** catch up with **your own sense of possibility**. You've explored, written, colored, pondered, and maybe even surprised yourself a little.

What You've Gained (That's More Than Just Tech Skills)

You've not only unwrapped the mysteries of artificial intelligence... You've also:

- **Practiced lifelong learning** in the most delightful way
- **Challenged your assumptions** about what's "too

complicated."

- **Built confidence** where uncertainty once lived
- And maybe, just maybe..., you started thinking like a digital pioneer with a café latte in one hand and your AI assistant in the other.

More than tools or tricks, what you now carry with you is a mindset – a gentle confidence that says,

"I'm not afraid of this. I can explore, ask questions, and make this work for me."

And So... What Now?

As you close this workbook, remember: this isn't an ending. It's a soft landing place on a path that keeps unfolding.

Keep using what you've learned here to:

- Simplify your day
- Stay connected to your people
- Organize your world
- Or just have a little fun experimenting with this "clever robot magic."

And when in doubt? Flip back to a sticky note, color a page, or take one small step forward. The work you've done here is yours to revisit whenever you need it.

A Final Word from Me to You

Thank you for trusting me to walk beside you in this new digital territory. I hope this workbook felt more like a companion than a curriculum - something cozy, encouraging, and just cheeky enough to keep you smiling.

Remember: AI might be the assistant, but you are the boss. You bring the wisdom, the wit, and the life experience that no machine could ever replace.
So here's to you – brave learner, lifelong explorer, notebook scribbler, and resilient human.
Don't stop here. Keep wondering. Keep learning. And always, always make room for joy in the journey.

When you're ready to take the next step, pull up a chair at the ChatGPT Café – where your curiosity meets cozy conversation. ChatGPT for Beginners Over Fifty will be waiting to serve up friendly guidance, daily prompts, and a whole menu of exciting new possibilities.

With warmth and a wink,

Margaret

(Still cheering you on from the other side of the page.)

Sticky Note-To-Self
AI isn't magic—it's just clever math in a fancy suit. Don't be fooled by the sparkle.

Breadcrumbs

*****REVIEW

YES You REALLY Did It!

You've now got everything you need to jump right into the fascinating world of AI – boots, brains, and all! Whether you're impressing the grandkids with tech talk or finally feeling at home in a digital world that once felt like Mars, you're officially rocking it.

But wait... you're not done yet (don't worry, no homework involved)!

You can help others take that same exciting first step by sharing your thoughts about this book on Amazon. Your review might be the exact nudge someone else over fifty needs to say, "Well, if they can do it, maybe I can too!"

Think of it as leaving a trail of breadcrumbs – or better yet, chocolate chip cookies – for fellow explorers.

By leaving a quick review, you're helping to:

- Spark curiosity and confidence in other beginners
- Keep the AI magic going strong
- Build a friendly, supportive community of learners

Thank you for being part of the journey.
The real magic of AI happens when we share what we've learned- and thanks to you, that spark is spreading.

Please leave your honest review on the Platform where you found this book or click the link below:
https://www.amazon.com/review/review-your-purchases/?asin=1923524003

With gratitude (and possibly a celebratory dance),
Margaret Fields

BONUS Chapter

A Moment to Color, Connect & Unwind

Before you close the workbook, we've saved something special just for you. Tucked into the back, you'll find a collection of calming adult coloring pages – designed to soothe the mind, spark a little creativity, and offer a well-earned pause. And because learning is even sweeter when shared, we've added a few kid-friendly pages too – perfect for coloring alongside a grandchild, a friend, or just for the joy of it. So grab your pencils, take a breath, and enjoy this quiet moment. You've earned it!

Made in United States
North Haven, CT
05 November 2026

21772056R00059